A SKETCHBOOK

BY E.C.

EUGENE ST. MARTIN, JR.

iUniverse®

A SKETCHBOOK BY E.C.

iUniverse books may be ordered through booksellers or by contacting:

iUniverse
1663 Liberty Drive
Bloomington, IN 47403
www.iuniverse.com
1-800-Authors (1-800-288-4677)

ISBN: 978-1-5320-1880-0 (sc)
ISBN: 978-1-5320-1829-9 (e)

Print information available on the last page.

iUniverse rev. date: 03/01/2017

This book is dedicated to my family, friends, fellow workers, and to all the people who have helped me in my life. It is especially dedicated to our students. I am thankful to have the opportunity to work with them as well as all the ones in the past years. And this book is dedicated to Liz and Clay Dickson. Furthermore this book is dedicated to God. Thank you.

E. C.

REFERENCES

Gallwey, W. Timothy, Inner Tennis, New York, New York: Random House, Inc. 1976.

Parent, Joe and Scanlon, Bill, Zen Tennis, USA, 2015.

Provance, Jake and Provance, Keith, Keep Calm and Trust God - Vol. 2, Tulsa, Oklahoma: Word and Spirit Publishing, 2015.

Stop,
slow down,
see God,
be content with what
    I have.

"As you take time to get to know God personally through prayer and His word, Faith will come alive in your heart." from "<u>Keep Calm</u> And <u>Trust</u> <u>in</u> <u>God</u>."
Jake Provance
and Keith Provance

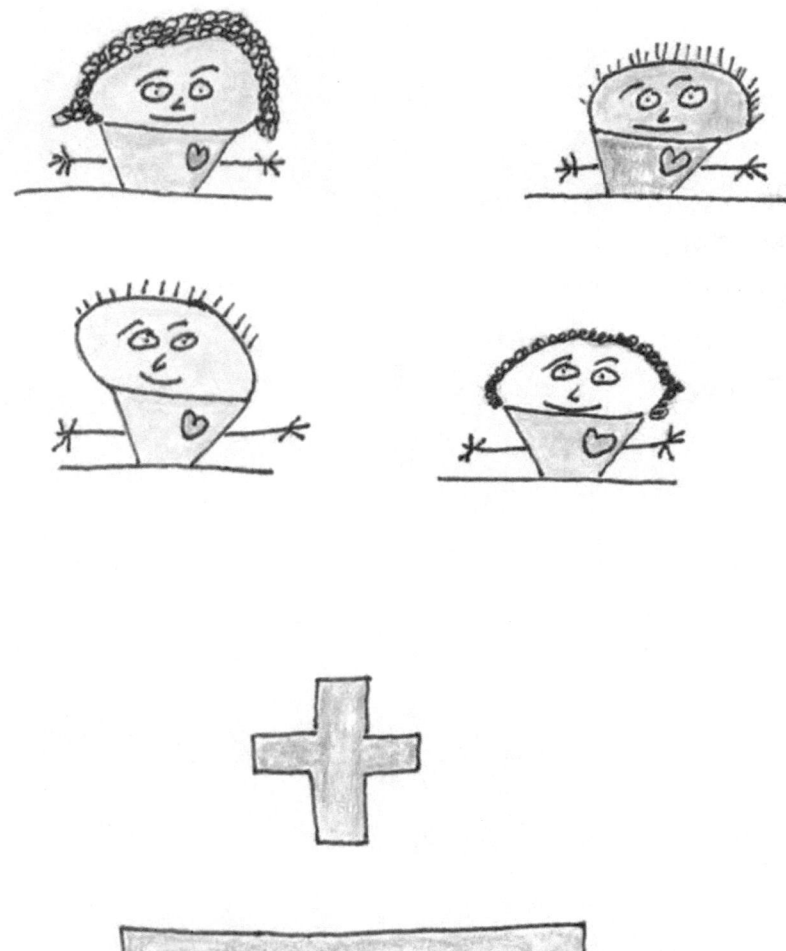

from church

Father Bob "... take the long picture ... looking through God's eyes in how God sees me."

Father Bob Stine

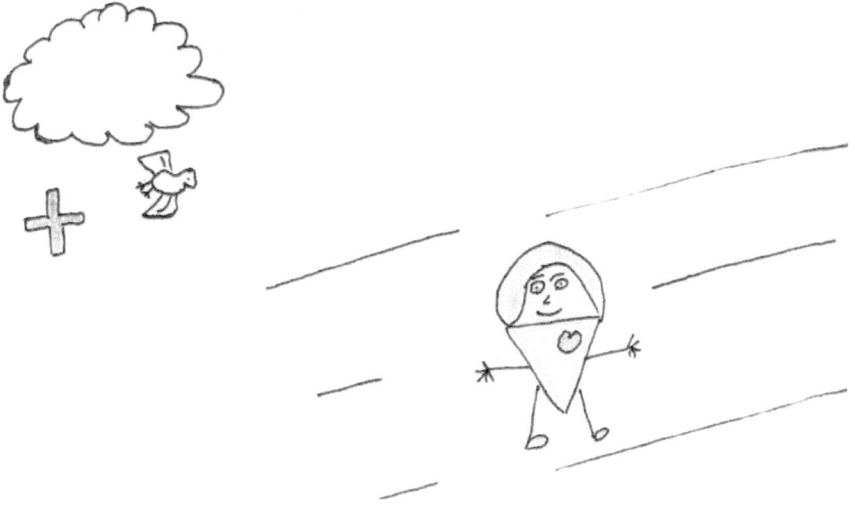

to be open to other people
and this time to love God,
a focus on that.

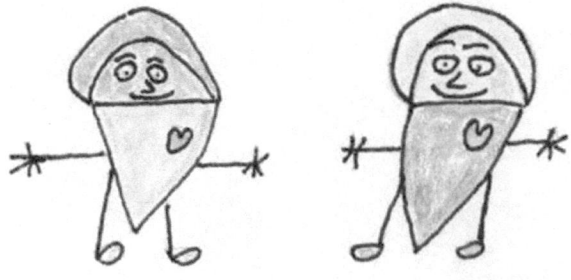

I must make peace otherwise I cause my body to cough.

I breathe in. I breathe out.

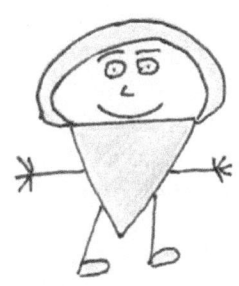 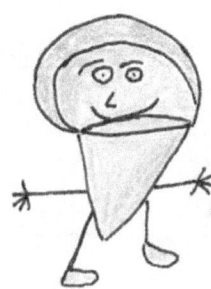

I listen to my
breathing.
I trust in God.
I breathe in,
I breathe out,
I listen.

to love God and to love all of creation,
to go to Communion to be with God
rather than just to get something.

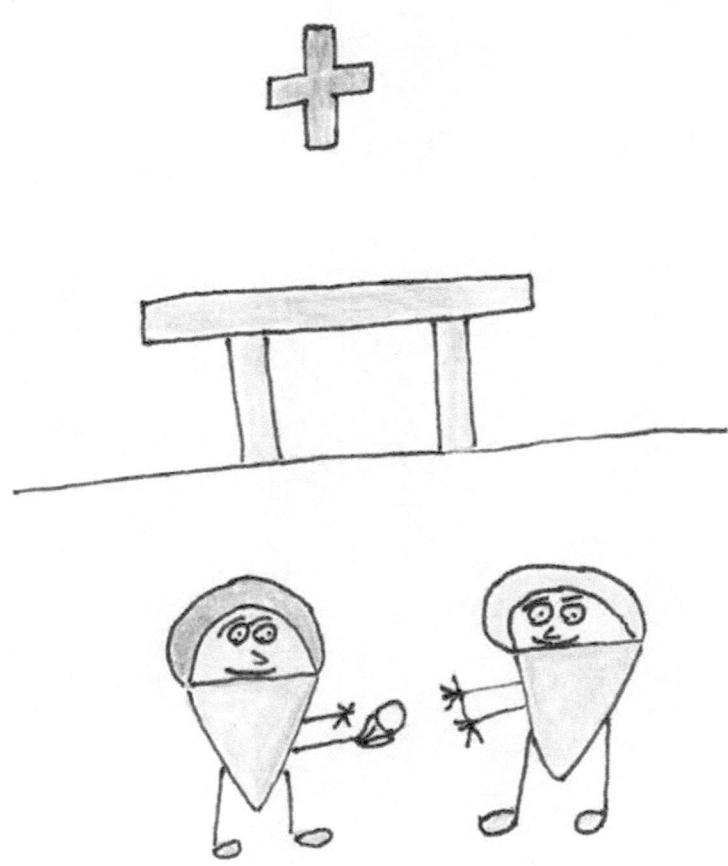

to love God
and to love others today
with the means I do have.
And let God guide me,
let Jesus guide me today.
Listen.
Whole purpose to love God
and others today with what
    I have.

May I be grateful and thankful
and love You with all my heart.

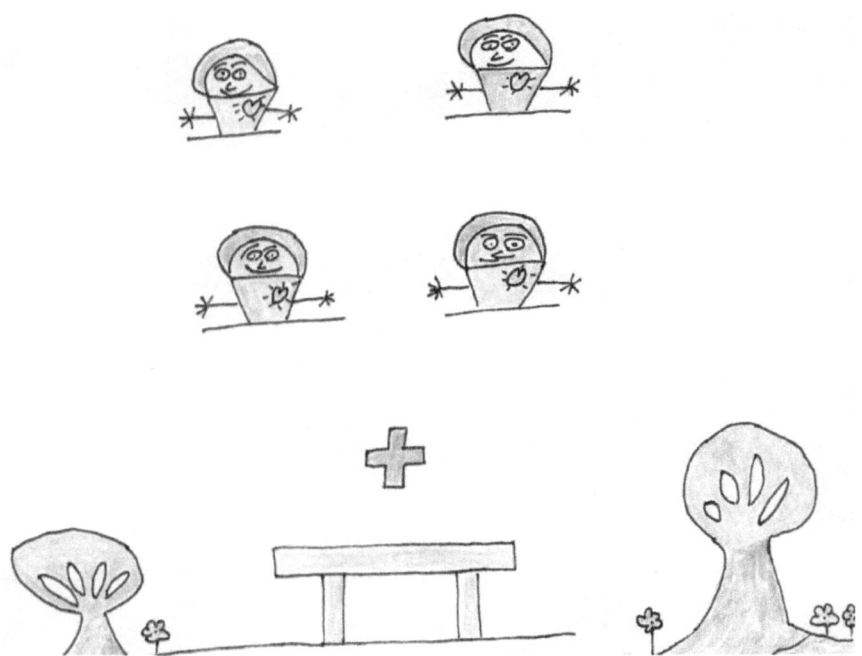

go out and see the world

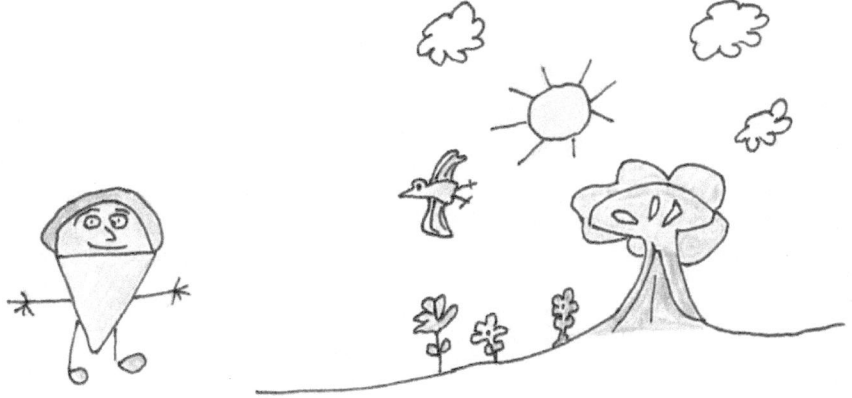

Maybe write something very
sacred and beautiful.

It comes through me,
the pictures and stories.

We are all broken,
We all make mistakes.
It is the whole.
We are all broken.
We are all part of the whole.

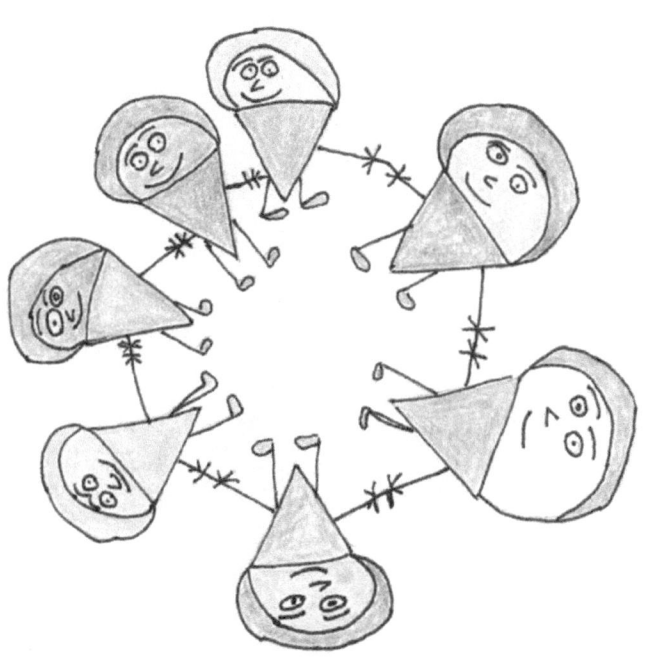

a moderate life,
simple,
refrain from looking under certain rocks
for things like fame and attention,
instead look towards God and the cross.
Let go of certain attachments,
    there will be more of a chance for peace.

My life,
keep it simple and
serve.
My life, my teaching
simple and serve.
With a friend,
no fair so obsessive, in control.
Simple and serve.

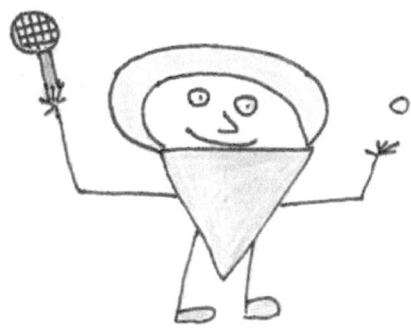

Jesus saves
God saves
pray to God.

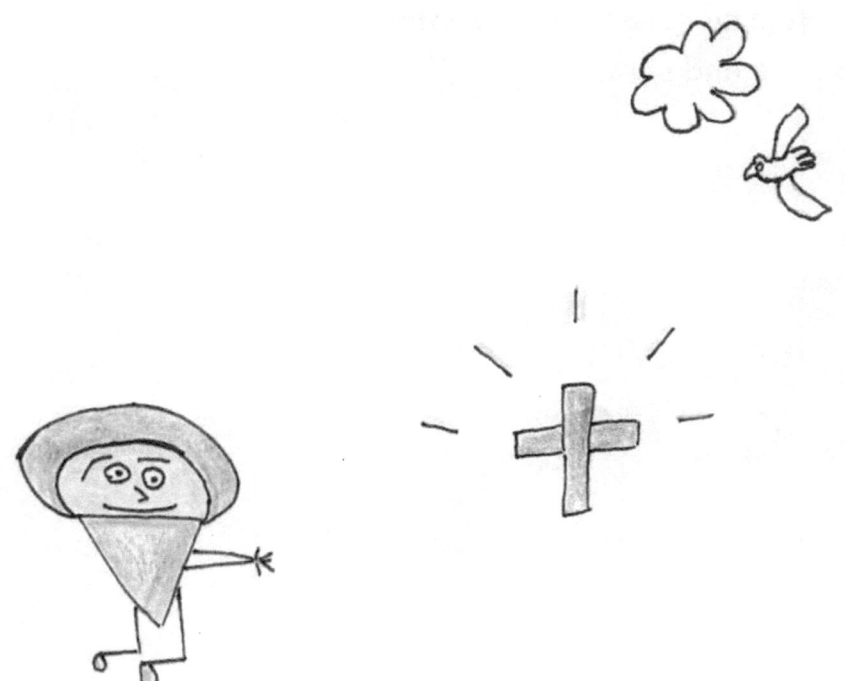

From "Zen Tennis"

"You just need to undo the interference and unleash the talent that is already there."

"Trusting your swing ... means you'll let your body do its best to produce the balance and rhythm you've trained in practice."

"Fill your mind with images of the shots you want to hit and your body will swing the racket without self-consciously thinking how to do it."

Dr. Joe Parent and Bill Scanlon

It is the journey,
so too in our practices, play,
    and our life.

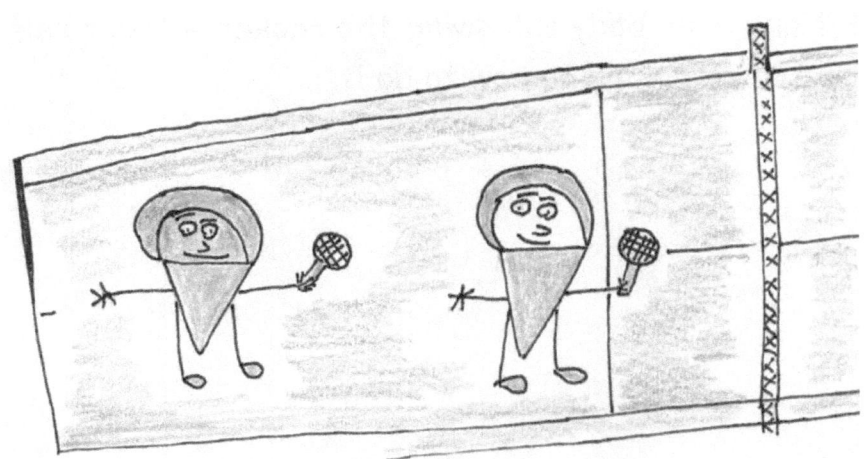

From "Zen Tennis"

"Well said, Ishi, "Since I was little I was taught to always be more curious than afraid."

"Like Ishi, you can take an attitude of curiosity and courage instead of fearing what you might encounter."

"When a point is done, it's done. Focus on the only point that matters: the one you're playing now."

Dr. Joe Parent and Bill Scanlon

do something for someone else - cut the grass.

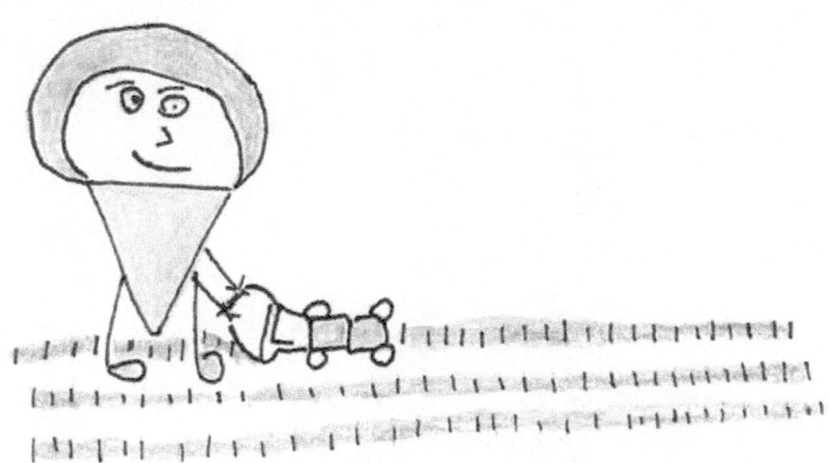

I owe a lot of people things, for example Ron.

Thank you.

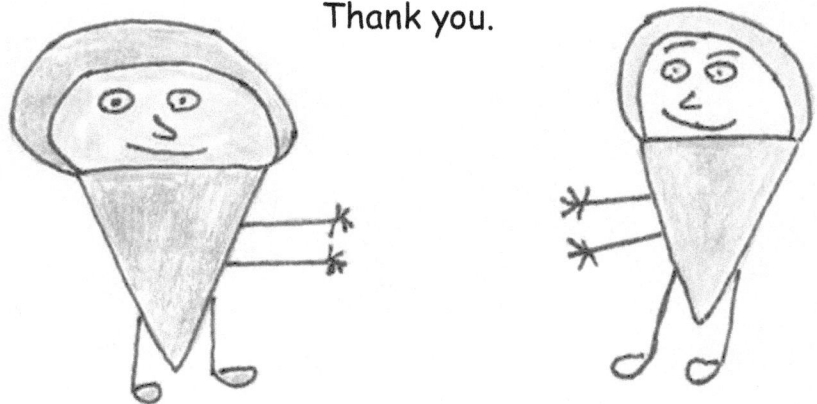

From church – Father Josh Johnson
    Father Josh said that when we fall in love with God,
        He will clean me, He will change me.

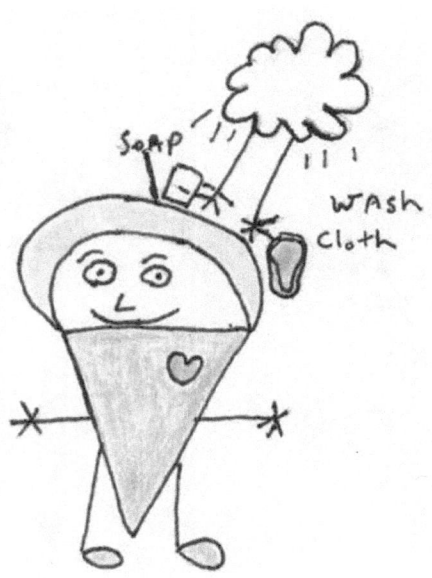

I need to leave things up to God now.

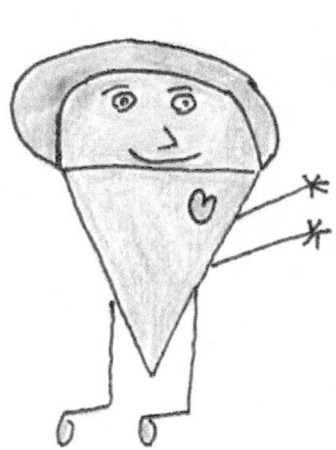

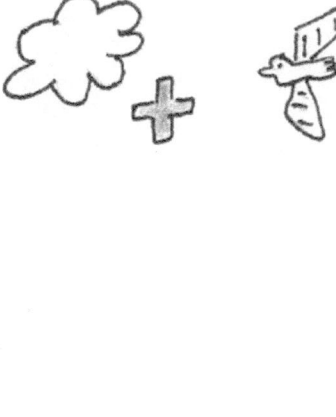

What is important?
  be present,
  be sincere,
  a true heart,
  a loving heart.

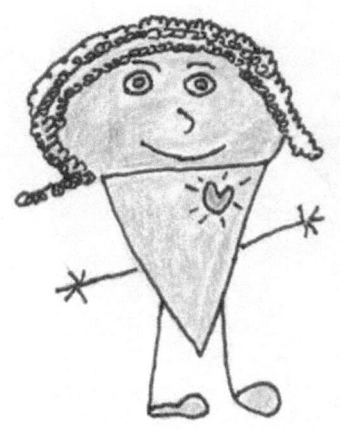

to be real

to be sincere.
It is the journey.
One's internal motivation.
"Where there is a will,
there is a way."

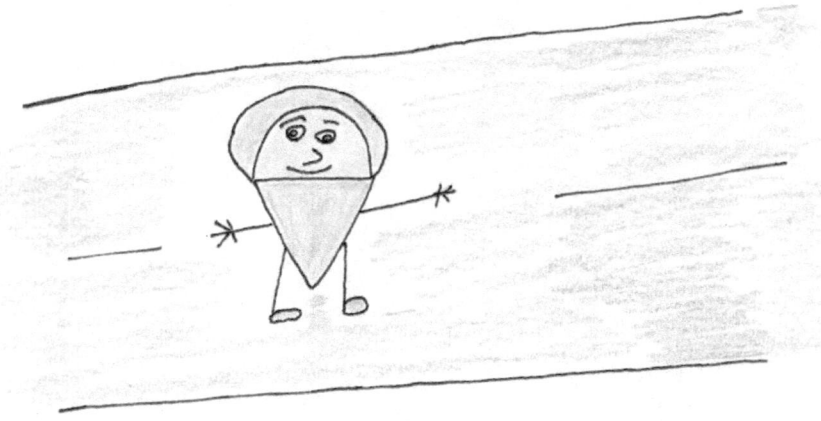

When a person uses "bounce, hit" they can play with anyone. This means they say "bounce" when the ball bounces on their side of the court and they say "hit" when they contact the ball. They do the same for when the ball bounces on their opponent's side of the court. They say "bounce" when the ball bounces and "hit" when the ball is hit.

Also when a person quietens the coaching tips and focuses on the seams of the ball.... when he notices the seams of the ball and breathes at contact it is pleasurable to play.

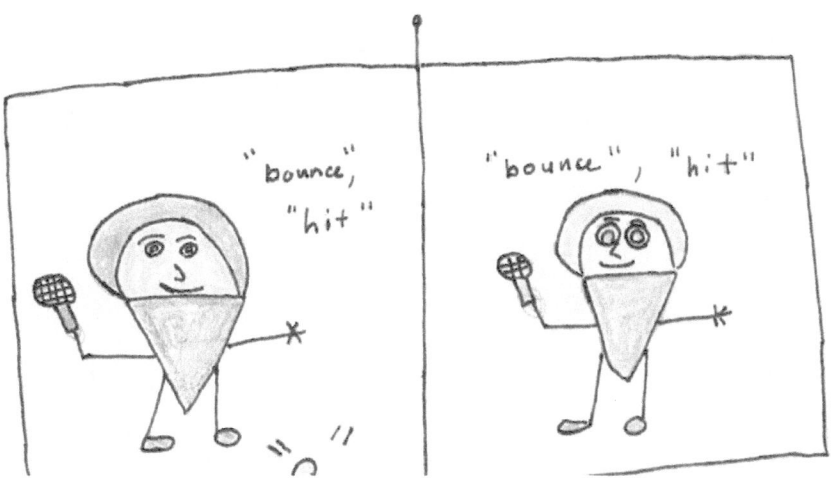

to tend to this day.

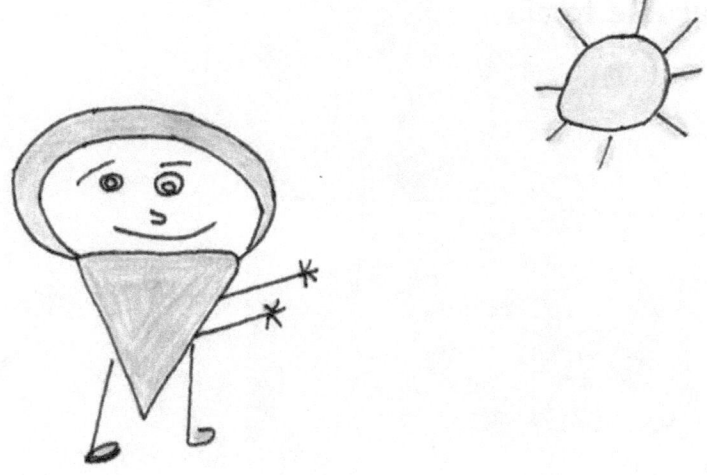

to serve.

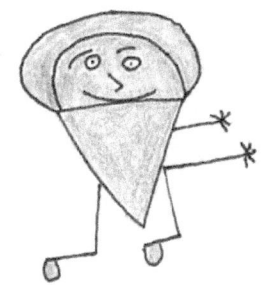

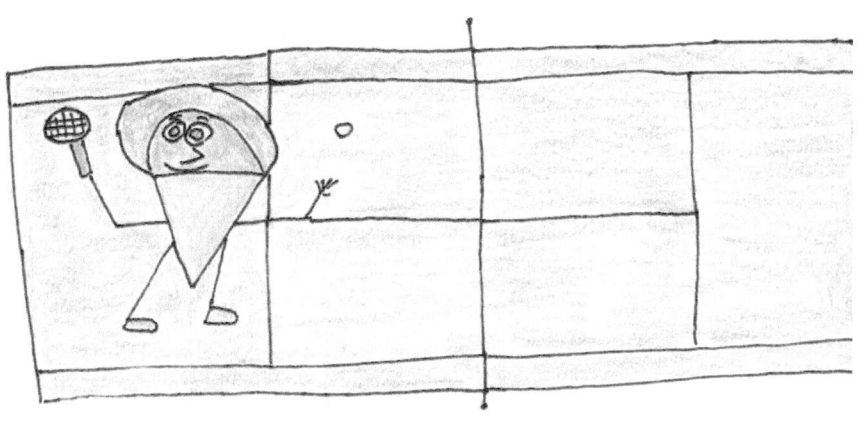

Clean my own home first.

Recycle my life.

I love seeing the beauty of nature
   and being out with nature.

Better to give in a quiet way
   like Liz does than all the profound ideas.

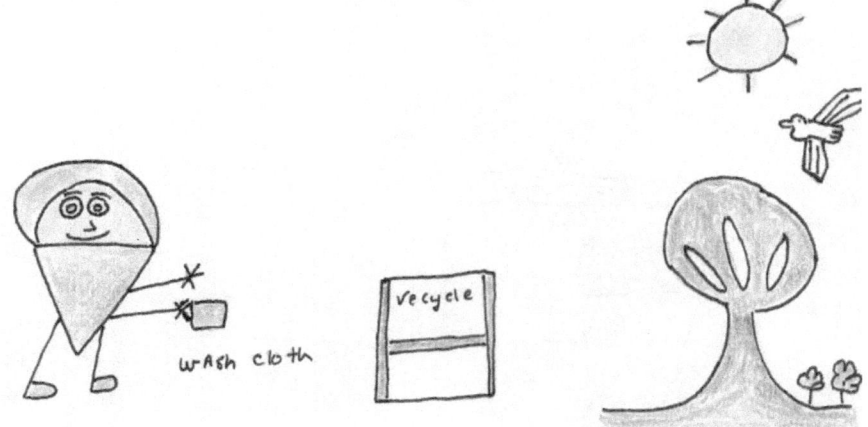

About our response.

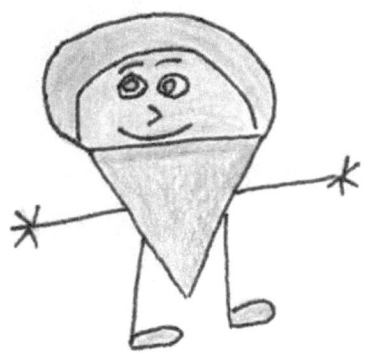

breathing in,
breathing out,
deep beneath one's belly
button,
calm.

time to listen.

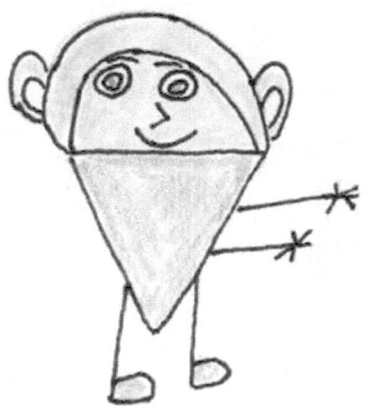 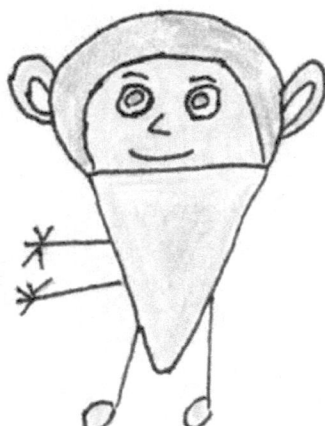

there are so many kids out there
to bring God's love to... so many orphans.

I need to keep writing..

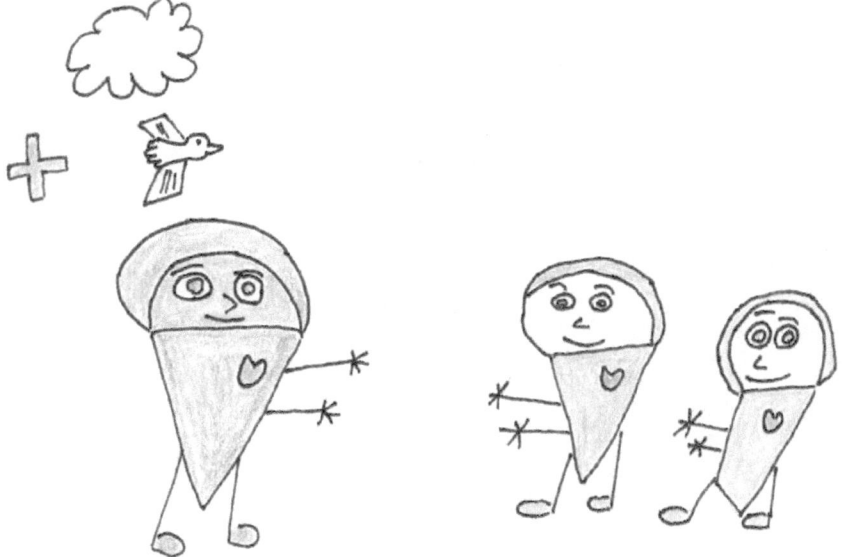

Needs to be
in the little bitty things,
my life,
or else I get overwhelmed.

"little bitty steps"

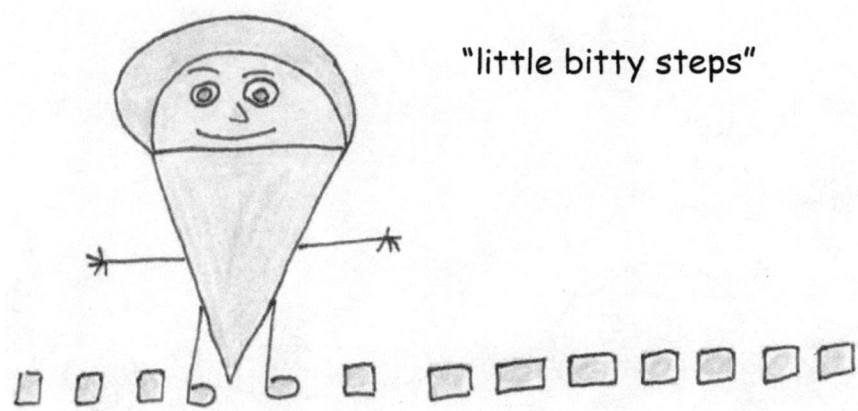

I look for someone to be for me.
Instead I need to be for others.

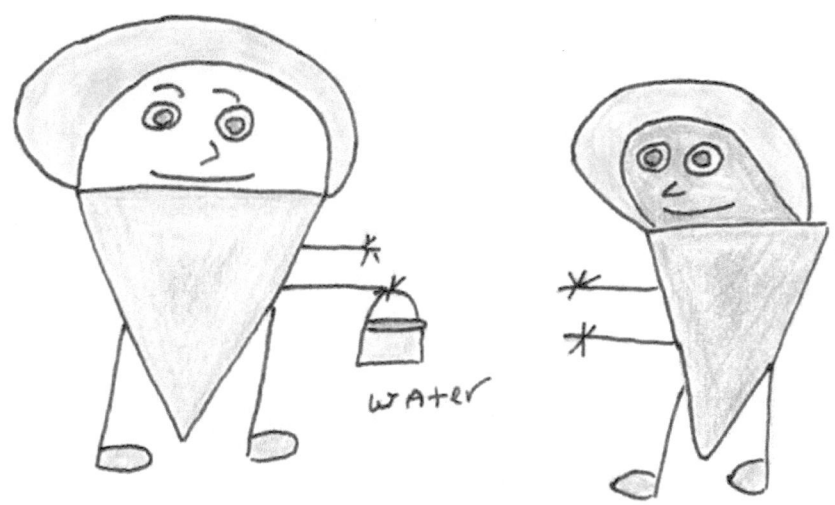

Dear God,

　　May I be an instrument of Your love today for these kids. May I be a conduit bringing Your love to others.
　　That is the key. That is the purpose. Thank You for letting me see that.

E. C.

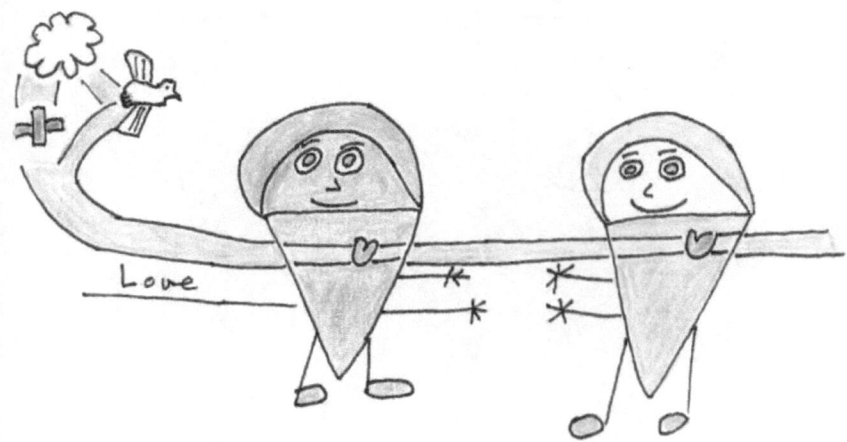

A life based on stimulus response

     vs. I choose

     vs. I chart my own course

     vs. what God offers

     vs. what Jesus offers.

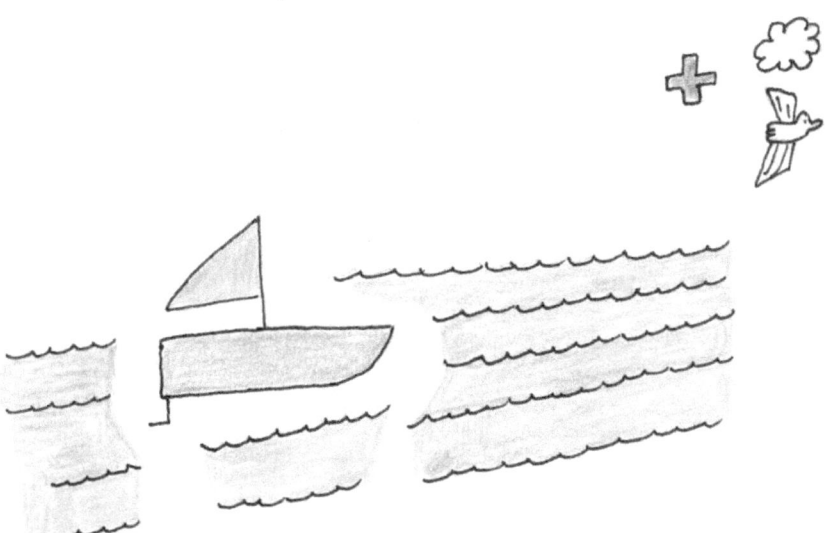

for the safety of the kids and adults.

to pray the rosary,
to do my back exercises.

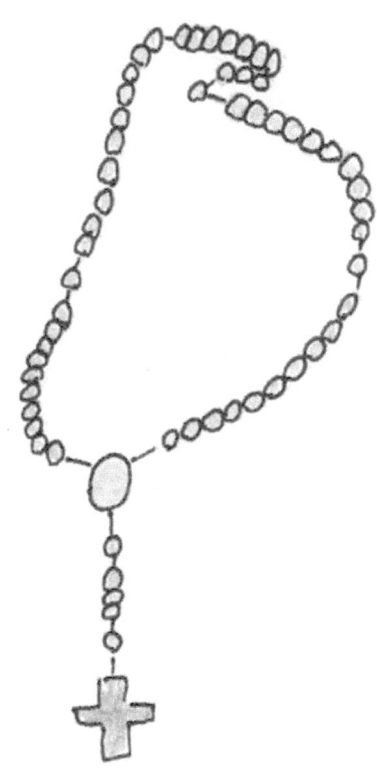

THIS MOMENT   vs.   looking down the road in
                       fear.

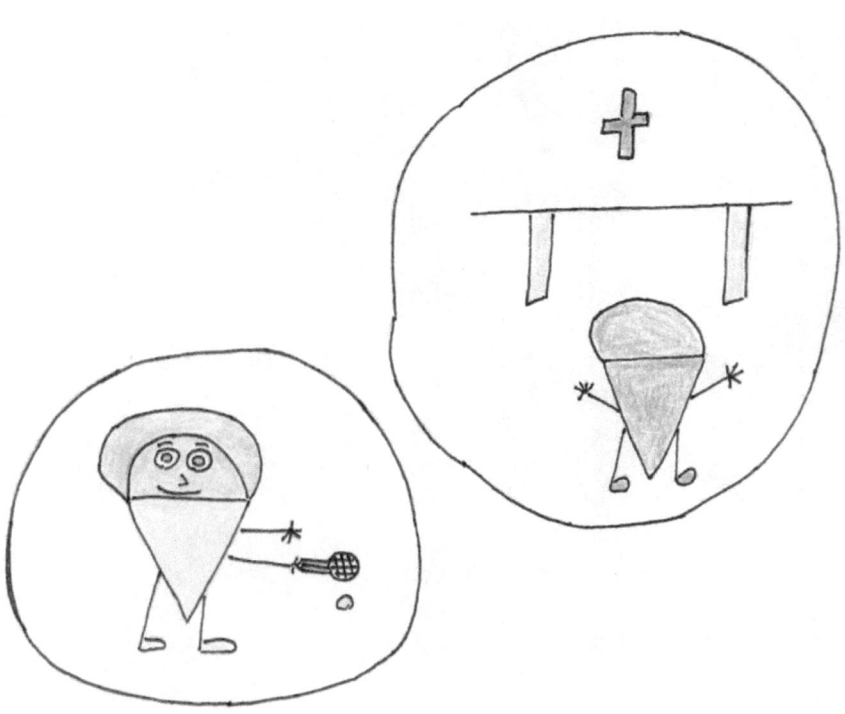

On my knees and work,
serve and return,
this moment,
this day.

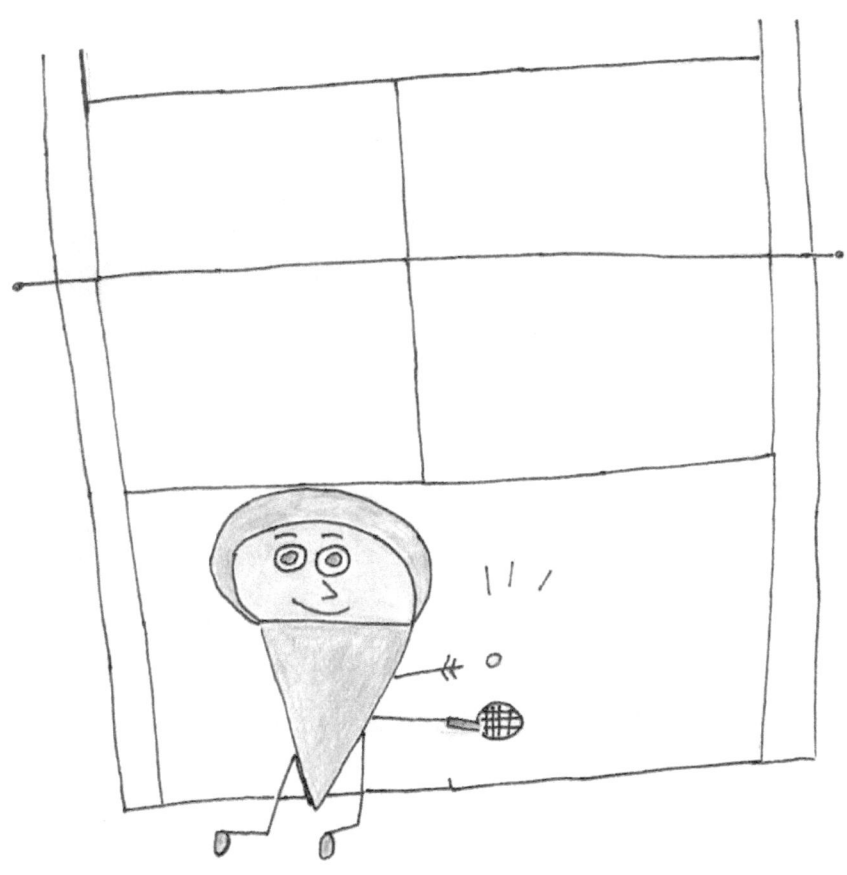

that which is in front of me,
the people God has brought us.

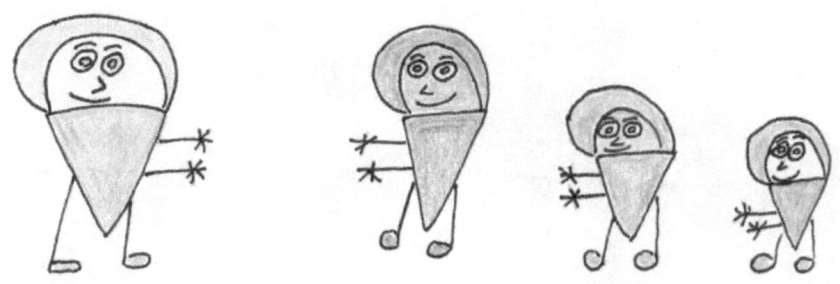

being in this present moment.

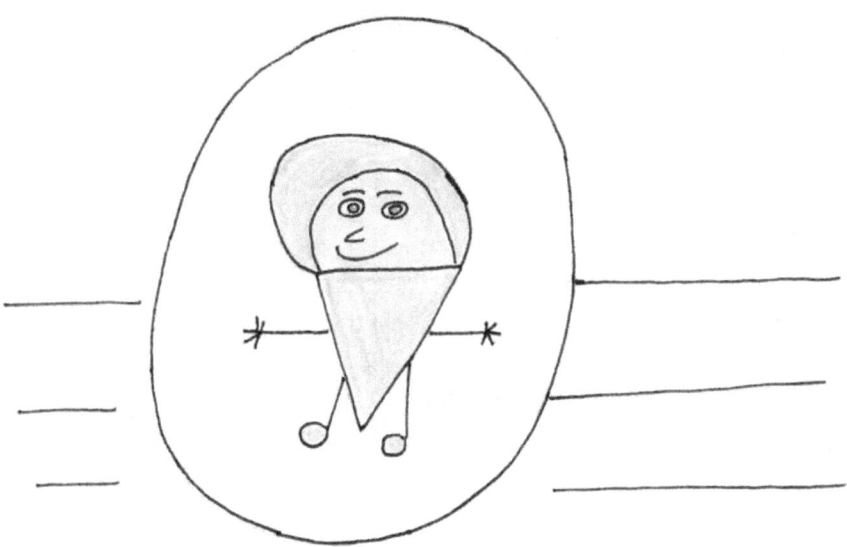

Jesus saves
God saves
pray to God.

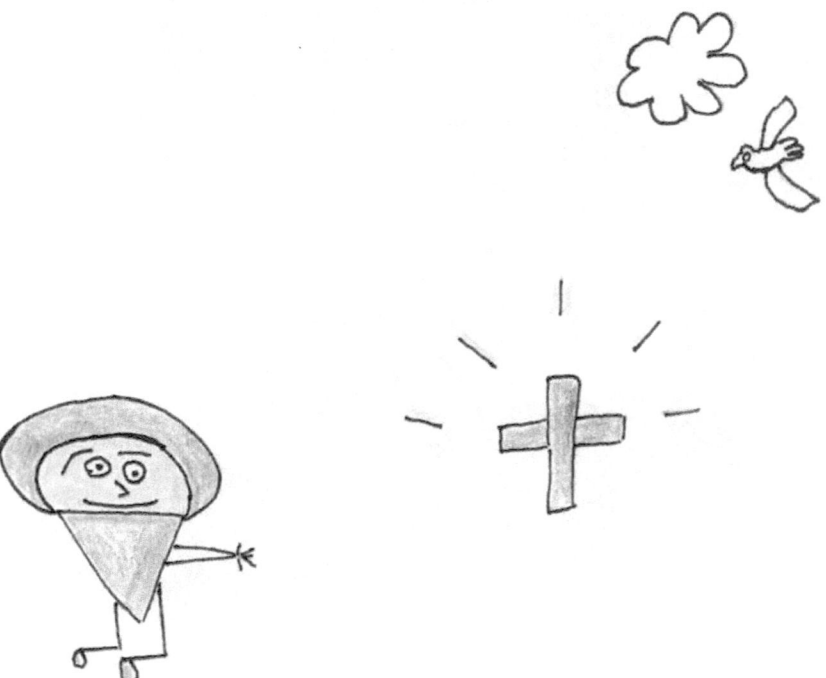

rally,
now to a target,
"bounce, hit,"
notice where the ball
goes in relation to the target,
notice again,
notice again,
notice again,
without getting beady eyed.

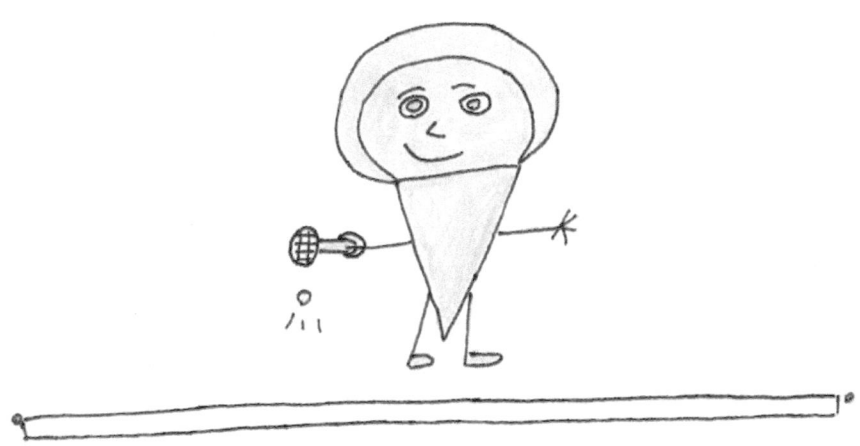

love is a bigger picture than me, it is about others and all of creation vs. centered on me.

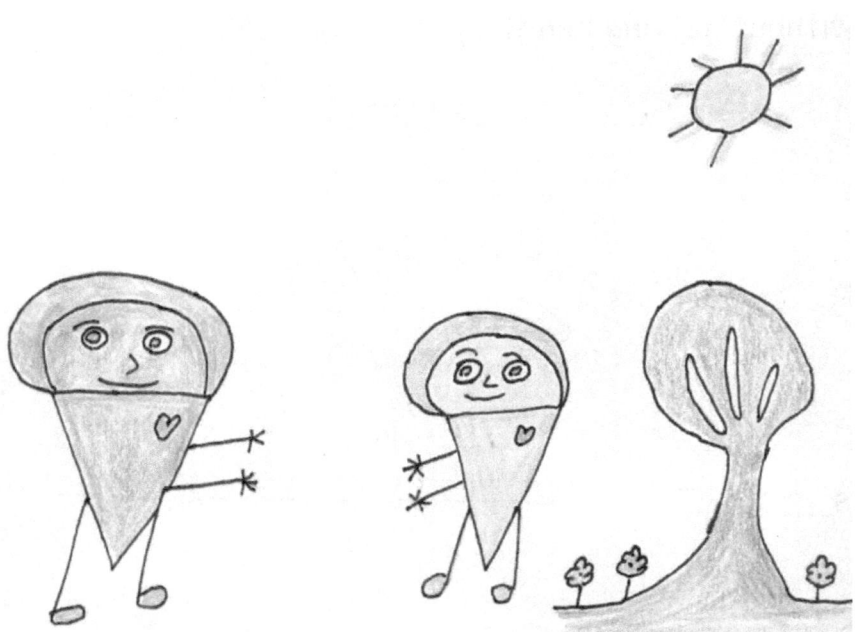

May I be thankful for the people life brings me.

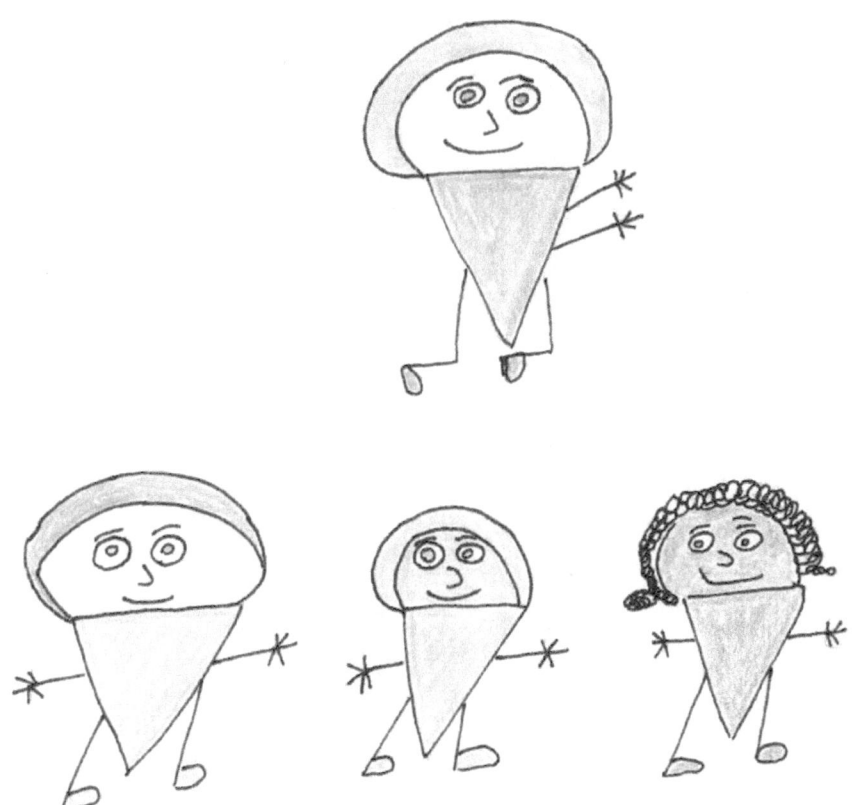

the most important thing in my life ... to be here, to be here, to be right where I am ... to see the people I am with now... to be happy with what I have now.

May I love You God in all I do today ... tend to with love.

All for God.
Everything we do for God.

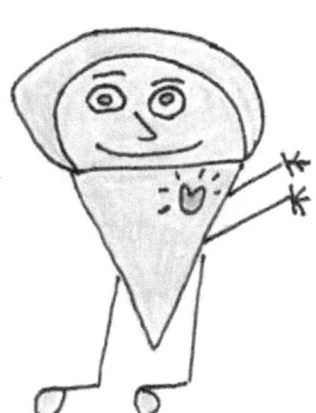

tennis - teaching, playing and my life,
sincere,
get on my knees and serve.
tend to with love.
My classes,
open my heart
And get on my knees.

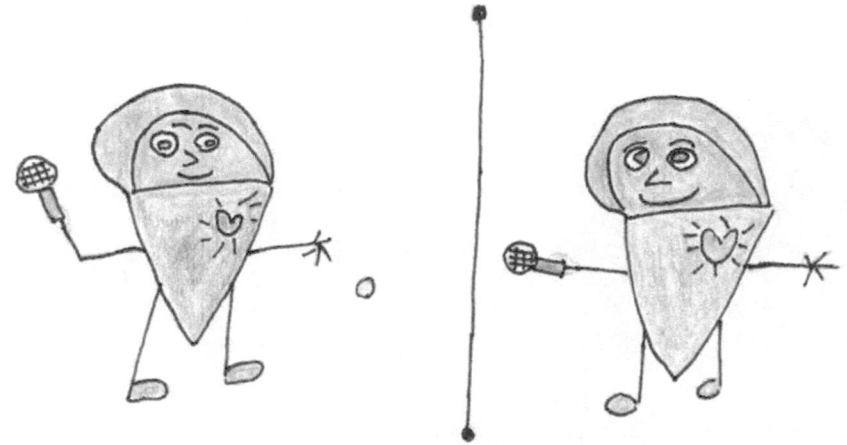

to live my life in Harmony with God,
to live my life in Beauty with God,
to become that Harmony,
to become that Beauty,
to become Love.

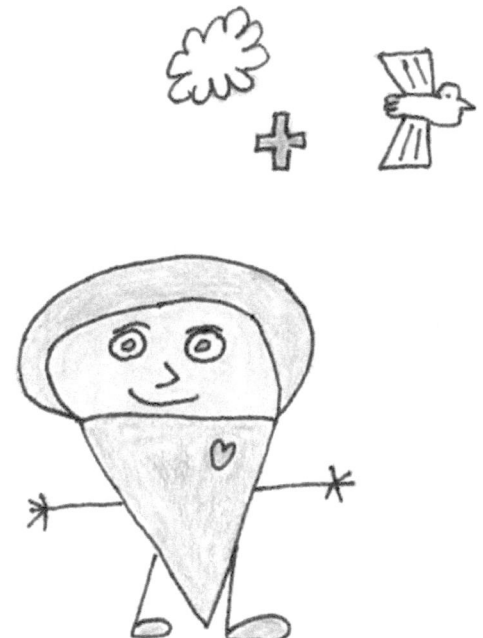

www.ingramcontent.com/pod-product-compliance
Lightning Source LLC
Chambersburg PA
CBHW021041180526
45163CB00005B/2224